Little Pebble™ **Celebrate Winter**

All About
Christmas

by Martha E. H. Rustad

CAPSTONE PRESS
a capstone imprint

Little Pebble is published by Capstone Press,
1710 Roe Crest Drive, North Mankato, Minnesota 56003
www.capstonepub.com

Library of Congress Cataloging-in-Publication Data
Rustad, Martha E. H. (Martha Elizabeth Hillman), 1975– author.
  All about Christmas / by Martha E. H. Rustad.
     pages cm.—(Little pebble. Celebrate winter)
  Summary: "Simple nonfiction text and full-color photographs present
the winter holiday of Christmas"—Provided by the publisher.
  Audience: Ages 5–7
  Audience: K to grade 3
  Includes bibliographical references and index.
  ISBN 978-1-4914-6006-1 (library binding)—ISBN 978-1-4914-6018-4 (pbk.)
  ISBN 978-1-4914-6030-6 (ebook pdf)
  1. Christmas—Juvenile literature. I. Title.
  BV45.R87 2016
  394.2663—dc23   2015001846

Editorial Credits
Erika L. Shores, editor; Cynthia Della-Rovere, designer;
Tracy Cummins, media researcher; Tori Abraham, production specialist

Photo Credits
Getty Images: Robert Nicholas, 15; iStockphoto: SeanShot, 21,
Thomas_EyeDesign, 19; Shutterstock: Air Images, 9, Aleksei Potov, cover,
I love photo, 7, oliveromg, 5, sellingpix, Design Element, Timmary, 1,
Valentina Proskurina, 3; SuperStock: Design Pics, 11; Thinkstock: Fuse, 13,
Stockbyte, 17.

Printed in the United States of America in North Mankato, Minnesota.
032015   008823CGF15

Table of Contents

Getting Ready

Christmas is coming!

What are some ways

to get ready?

Sam and Mia decorate.

They hang lights on a tree.

Tyler and Ana bake.
They help Dad
make treats.

8

Liam helps others.

He serves food at a shelter.

La! Gabby sings.
She knows the words
to many carols.

Time with Family

Maria goes to church.

She sits with her family.

Alexis visits.

Her family goes to

Grandma's house.

Taylor gives gifts.
She wraps a toy
for her sister.

Counting the Days

Three, two, one!

James counts down the days.

How do you celebrate Christmas?

Glossary

carol—a song people sing at Christmas

celebrate—to honor a special event

Christmas—a holiday Christians celebrate to honor the birth of Jesus

church—a place people go to pray, sing, and worship

shelter—a place that helps needy people by giving them food and a place to sleep

wrap—to put paper or cloth around a gift

Read More

Felix, Rebecca. *We Celebrate Christmas in Winter*. Let's Look at Winter. Ann Arbor, Mich.: Cherry Lake Pub., 2014.

Landau, Elaine. *What Is Christmas?* I Like Holidays! Berkeley Heights, N.J.: Enslow, 2012.

Pettiford, Rebecca. *Christmas*. Holidays. Minneapolis: Jump!, 2015.

Internet Sites

FactHound offers a safe, fun way to find Internet sites related to this book. All of the sites on FactHound have been researched by our staff.

Here's all you do:
Visit *www.facthound.com*
Type in this code: 9781491460061

Super-cool stuff! Check out projects, games and lots more at
www.capstonekids.com

Index